W9-BMQ-942

NATIONAL GEOGRAPHIC

On the Menu

PIONEER EDITION

By Susan E. Goodman

CONTENTS

What Is This? *A sea dragon looks like a piece of seaweed. This helps the sea dragon hide.*

On the Menu

By Susan E. Goodman

Is that seaweed? No, it is a sea dragon. The way it looks helps it hide in the water. That is one of many animal tricks for staying alive.

© JAMES D. WATT, STEPHENFRINKCOLLECTION.COM (DRAGON); ARTVILLE LLC (SILVERWARE); © PAR BRANNON/NATUREPL.COM, NATUREPL.COM FROM WWW.NATUREPL (WASP)

Master of Disguise

A **predator** is an animal that eats other animals. Most predators cannot eat what they cannot see. To stay safe, many animals hide.

Some animals hide by blending in. That is just what the leafy sea dragon does.

The sea dragon has skin that looks like leaves. The skin makes the dragon look like seaweed. It is a water plant.

The dragon's small fins also help it hide. They slowly push the dragon through the water. So the sea dragon looks like a piece of floating seaweed.

Hungry predators stay away from seaweed—and sea dragons.

Show-offs!

The leafy sea dragon hides to stay safe. Other animals want predators to see them. They stay safe by showing off their bright colors.

Scientists call these **warning colors.** The bright colors tell predators to stay away.

You have probably seen warning colors. For example, what do you do when an insect flies by? Do you swat it? Maybe.

What happens when a yellow bug flies in your face? Do you swat it? No. Yellow is a warning color. It tells you the bug might be a bee or wasp. It could sting you if you hit it.

Rolling Rolling Rolling...

1 After spotting a predator, an armadillo first tries to run away. If that does not work, the armadillo stops.

2 Then the armadillo begins to tuck itself into a ball. It folds its head and legs inside its shell.

South African grasshopper

Some grasshoppers have red and blue warning colors. They also make foam. It tastes awful.

When predators see the warning colors, they remember the yucky foam. They eat something else.

On the Ball

Some animals need more protection. They wear armor. It protects them. It also makes them harder to eat.

The armadillo has two ways to stay safe. It has a tough shell. You might think that the shell is enough protection. It is not.

This animal tries to run away from danger. If that does not work, it tucks in its legs and ears. Then it rolls into a ball.

Most hungry hunters do not know how to eat a rolled-up armadillo. They can poke at it. But they cannot find a way through the shell. Without a tasty bite to eat, they move on.

© MARK PAYNE-GILL, NATUREPL.COM (ARMADILLOS); © AUGUST SYCHOLT, AGE FOTOSTOCK AMERICA (GRASSHOPPER)

Finally the armadillo tucks its tail next to its head. Now the shell covers the animal's whole body.

4 After rolling itself into a ball, the armadillo is safe. Predators cannot find a tasty bite to eat.

Lying Lizard

The frilled lizard has another way to stay off the menu. It runs away. That does not always work. It sometimes has to bluff its way out of danger.

The lizard opens its mouth. It hisses and fluffs out its neck. It also whips its long tail around. This makes the lizard look big and scary.

These moves can scare predators away. The predators look for another meal. The lizard lives. It gets to look for its own tasty snacks.

School Safety

Other animals find safety in numbers. That is why many fish live in groups, or **schools.** At the first sign of trouble, schooling fish swim as close together as they can. This makes it hard for predators to catch a meal.

Common Defenses

These are just a few of the ways that animals stay off of the menu. You can spot many other ways. Look at your pets. How do they stay safe?

The frilled lizard looks harmless most of the time.

When a predator comes close, the lizard spreads the skin around its neck. It tries to scare the predator away.

Before

After

A.NORTHCOTT, CORBIS (BEFORE); © KLAUS UHLENHUT, ANIMALS ANIMALS/EARTH SCENES (AFTER);
PERRINE, SEAPICS.COM (SHARK); PHOTODISC (LADYBUG)

See Food? *This tiger shark has plenty to eat. Or does it? Fish are harder to catch in schools.*

Wordwise

predator: animal that eats other animals

school: large group of fish

warning color: bright color that warns predators to stay away

Crocodile

Eye-Teasing Tricks

Death adder

Animals have lots of ways to hide from predators. Did you know that predators have tricks of their own? They hide to catch their dinner!

A Bump on a Log

That is true for the crocodile. It hides in water. It can lie very still for hours. Only its eyes and nose show above the water. Blink. It looks around. It watches for food.

The crocodile's skin is bumpy. In the water, it looks like a floating log. Yet this "log" bites. An animal comes near. The croc leaps up and eats it.

Trick or Treat

A death adder is another sneaky predator. This snakes uses a trick to catch its meals.

A death adder is mostly brown. It blends in with the ground. It hides under leaves and grass. Its coloring makes it hard to see.

But the death adder does not hide its tail. Why not? The tip of its tail looks like a worm. Small animals see this "worm." They want to eat it, so they come closer. Then the death adder strikes.

MICHAEL NICHOLS (CROCODILE); MICHAEL & PATRICIA FOGDEN/CORBIS (DEATH ADDER).

Awesome Adaptations

Animals have many ways to stay safe. Their colors and shapes can make them hard to see. Look at the photos. What helps these animals stay safe?

1 Where are the animals in each picture?

2 How would you describe the place where each animal lives?

3 Why are the animals hard to find?

4 How would you describe the color and shape of each animal?

5 How do the color and shape of each animal help it survive?

Snowshoe hare

Snake

Insects

Lizard

Spider

Tree frog

JCE DALE (SNOWSHOE HARE); CHRIS JOHNS (SNAKE); PAUL A. ZAHL (INSECTS); ROBERT SISSON (SPIDER, LIZARD, TREE FROG).

Animal Meals

Answer these questions to get a taste of what you have learned.

1 How do some animals stay safe?

2 Why can bright colors help keep an animal safe?

3 How do some animals try to scare off predators?

4 How can hiding help predators catch a meal?

5 How can an animal's color and shape help it survive?